Read-Aloud Plays

Heroes in American History

by Tracey West and Katherine Noll

SCHOLASTIC
PROFESSIONAL BOOKS

New York • Toronto • London • Auckland • Sydney
Mexico City • New Delhi • Hong Kong • Buenos Aires

Cover design by Josué Castilleja

Interior design by Sydney Wright

Cover illustrations and interior illustrations by Holly Jones

ISBN: 0-439-22264-8

3 4 5 6 7 8 9 10   40   09 08 07 06 05 04

Contents

Introduction

One of the most interesting and inspiring tasks an elementary school teacher is charged with is to introduce to his or her students the men and women who helped make the United States great. Most children first learn about such important figures as George Washington or Dr. Martin Luther King, Jr. in the early grades, and carry those facts and impressions with them throughout their lives.

In this book we've singled out fifteen famous American heroes likely to be familiar faces in your classroom. You'll find a short read-aloud play about each American, along with helpful teaching information.

We hope you'll find that using read-aloud plays is a fun, exciting way to share the stories of these American heroes with your students.

—*Tracey West and Katherine Noll*

Why Use Read-Aloud Plays

Using read-aloud plays in the classroom is an excellent way to:

* ❈ build oral literacy skills and reading fluency.
* ❈ encourage listening skills.
* ❈ bring new life to familiar themes.
* ❈ draw out quiet or at-risk students.

About This Book

A quick glance at the table of contents will reveal that most of the fifteen famous American heroes we've chosen are people you normally work into your lesson plans. Others might be welcome additions to a tried-and-true theme, such as Women's History Month. We've listed theme connections under the title of each play to give you some ideas for how these plays can be incorporated into your curriculum.

Following each play is one page of material designed to help you share the play with your class. In each Teacher's Guide you'll find:

BACKGROUND: a collection of facts to introduce or follow up the play

ACTIVITY: an engaging, cross-curricular teaching idea to help broaden the play experience

WRITING PROMPT: a quick, fun suggestion to spur students to write something based on what they've read

DISCUSSION QUESTION: a simple question to get a classroom discussion going when the play is over

BOOK AND INTERNET LINKS: a bibliography of books and Web sites to enhance the excitement generated by the play

KEY VOCABULARY: an instant reference to introduce or review vocabulary

Using the Plays

Here are some simple guidelines for using the plays in your classroom:

✶ Look over the Teacher's Guide page before using each play to see if there are vocabulary words you wish to review, or ideas for introducing the play to the class.

✶ Use the character list at the start of each play to assign speaking roles. Feel free to cast girls in boys' parts and vice versa.

✶ Many of the plays are divided into two or more scenes. To make sure as many children as possible get a chance to speak, assign new roles each time the scene changes.

✶ Consider reviewing the Key Vocabulary listed in the Teacher's Guide before reading the play, so students won't stumble over unfamiliar words.

✶ Divide the class into small groups and have each group read the play aloud. Then reassemble the class for a post-play discussion and activity.

✶ Assign the plays as homework, encouraging students to read the play aloud with family members.

✶ Provide students with the books or Web site addresses listed after each play so they can learn more about the people who interest them.

✶ Remember that students truly enjoy read-aloud plays. Above all, have fun!

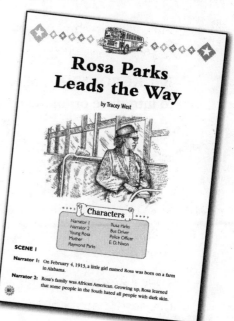

Squanto's Home

by Katherine Noll

Characters

Storyteller 1	Chief Massasoit
Storyteller 2	Samoset
Storyteller 3	Wampanoag Man
Storyteller 4	Wampanoag Woman
Captain Dermer	John Carver
Squanto	

SCENE 1

Storyteller 1: A long time ago, the only people who lived in America were the Native People.

Storyteller 2: A long time ago, the Native People lived in peace with the earth.

Storyteller 3: And a long time ago, it all changed.

Storyteller 4: People came on ships from faraway lands.

Storyteller 1: One day a ship came from England.

Storyteller 2: It sailed to the coast where the Patuxet (paw-TUX-et) and Wampanoag (WAHM-puh-NOH-ahg) tribes lived.

Storyteller 3: Men from the ship kidnapped people from these tribes.

Storyteller 4: They took them far away across the ocean.

Storyteller 1: Squanto (SKWAN-toh) was from the Patuxet tribe. He was kidnapped from his land.

Storyteller 2: He was taken to England. He lived there and learned to speak English.

Storyteller 3: But he always wanted to return to his home and his people.

Storyteller 4: And one day, he did.

SCENE 2

Captain Dermer: I need help, Squanto. I need to sail on the New England coast. I want to make a map. Many people from Europe and England want to go to this new land. They will need maps.

Squanto: What do you want me to do?

Captain Dermer: We will need supplies. The Native People are angry with us. They will not want to trade with us or help us. We want you to talk to them for us, Squanto.

Squanto: Why should I?

Captain Dermer: If you do this for us, we will take you back to your home.

Squanto: I will do it.

SCENE 3

Storyteller 1: Squanto and Captain Dermer traveled for many days. Soon they came to Squanto's home.

Squanto: My people! They are all dead! What has happened?

Captain Dermer: This is terrible. The entire Patuxet tribe is gone.

Storyteller 2: Squanto finally got to go home.

Storyteller 3: But all of his people were dead.

Storyteller 4: The village was empty.

Storyteller 1: Squanto was the only living Patuxet. He went to stay with another tribe, the Wampanoag.

Chief Massasoit: I am sorry, Squanto. The men from the ships brought a disease with them. It killed your people.

Squanto: All I wanted to do was come home. But now I have nothing.

Chief Massasoit: This will be your home. You will live with us.

SCENE 4

Storyteller 2: Squanto lived with the Wampanoag.

Storyteller 3: Although he was sad, he made a good friend named Samoset (SAM-oh-set).

Storyteller 4: Samoset was from the Algonquian (al-GON-kin) tribe.

Storyteller 1: Like Squanto, Samoset could speak English.

Storyteller 2: He learned it from the English men who came to fish and explore.

Squanto: Let's go hunting, Samoset. I know a good place to go near my old village.

Storyteller 3: The two friends went off.

Squanto: Let's stop and see my old home.

Samoset: Look! There are people here.

Squanto: They are English men and women. They have built homes here.

Samoset: What should we do?

Squanto: Let's ask Chief Massasoit (MASS-az-oh-it).

SCENE 5

Storyteller 4: Squanto and Samoset told Chief Massasoit what they had seen.

Storyteller 1: Many of the Wampanoag people were nervous.

Wampanoag Man: Do you think they are peaceful?

Wampanoag Woman: What if they have brought more disease with them?
My children could get sick.

Storyteller 2: Chief Massasoit sent Samoset to talk with the newcomers.
Samoset would find out if they were friendly.

Squanto: Samoset, what did the English people say?

Samoset: They call themselves Pilgrims. They want to make peace with us.
I need you to come back with me, Squanto.

Squanto: I will.

Storyteller 3: Squanto went back to his old home with Samoset.

Storyteller 4: But now Pilgrims were living there.

Storyteller 1: They named it Plymouth Colony.

John Carver: We would like to live in peace with our neighbors.

Squanto: We, too, want to live in peace.

John Carver: The Pilgrims need friends. It has been hard for us in Plymouth Colony. We don't have enough to eat.

Squanto: I can help teach you about this land. It was my home for many years.

Storyteller 2: Squanto taught the Pilgrims all about his home. He showed them where to fish.

Storyteller 3: And he taught them how to plant corn.

Storyteller 4: Without Squanto, the Pilgrims would not have survived in Plymouth Colony.

Storyteller 1: Squanto lived the rest of his life in Plymouth Colony. He got to go home after all.

The End

Squanto's Home

Background

Squanto, also known as Tisquantum, was born into the Patuxet tribe of Native Americans. They lived in present day Massachusetts and Rhode Island.

Although not much is known about Squanto's early life, it is believed he was kidnapped when he was in his early twenties by English explorers. After escaping from slavery, Squanto returned home to find his entire tribe dead, possibly from smallpox brought by European explorers.

In the spring of 1621, Squanto befriended the Pilgrims at Plymouth Colony. He gained eternal fame by helping the settlers find food, farm, and build homes. He died only a year after meeting the Pilgrims, in 1622.

Activity: Share Your Space

Mark off a square box by placing masking tape on the floor. (The size of the box will depend on the number of students participating.) Have one student stand in the box. Tell the student that this box is her home. One at a time, have other students enter the box. As they enter, they should announce that now this is their home too. Discuss the results with the class. What happened to the first student who "lived" in the box? Did her home grow smaller? Did she have to leave the box? What eventually happened to the Native People of America?

Writing Prompt

Squanto was kidnapped from his home and sailed to a faraway land. Imagine you are Squanto. Write a journal entry for the first night on the ship after you are kidnapped.

Discussion Question

The Pilgrims and Native Americans at first wanted to live in peace together. But it didn't last. What happened to the Native People after more newcomers came?

Links

 Tapenum's Day: A Wampanoag Indian Boy in Pilgrim Times by Kate Waters (Scholastic, 1996)

 The First Thanksgiving **http://teacher.scholastic.com/ thanksgiving/**

Key Vocabulary

Native People: many tribespeople in the United States prefer this term to *Native American*

Pilgrims: people who had received permission from the King of England to relocate to the New World

Busy Ben Franklin

by Tracey West

Characters

Narrator 1
Narrator 2
Sarah Franklin
Ben Franklin

James Franklin
Deborah Read
William Franklin
Thomas Jefferson

SCENE 1: Ben Franklin the Printer

Narrator 1: Benjamin Franklin was one of the men who founded the United States. But he did many other things, too.

Narrator 2: Benjamin Franklin was a printer, a scientist, and a statesman. And that's just the beginning!

Narrator 1: His printing career started in Boston, Massachusetts, in 1718, when he was only 12 years old.

Sarah Franklin: Where are you going, little brother?

Ben Franklin: I am off to see brother James at his print shop. I am going to learn how to be a printer.

Sarah: Don't you like working in father's candle shop?

Ben: I love to read. I want to improve my education. Learning how to be a printer will help me do both of those things.

Narrator 1: Benjamin worked for his brother James for five years. Then he decided to go off on his own.

James Franklin: Where are you going, little brother?

Ben: I have learned everything I can here. I want to go to Philadelphia.

Narrator 2: Ben started his own newspaper, the Philadelphia Gazette, in 1729.

Deborah Read: Where are you going, neighbor?

Ben: I must hurry to get out the next issue of the gazette.

Deborah: You are always in a hurry.

Ben: The sleeping fox catches no chickens, I always say.

Deborah: Your newspaper is very interesting. Why are there so many pictures and cartoons on the pages?

Ben: I believe that everyone should be able to understand the news, even if they can't read.

SCENE 2: Ben Franklin the Scientist

Narrator 1: Ben Franklin married Deborah Read in 1730.

Narrator 2: The next years were very busy for Benjamin Franklin. He stayed in the printing business. But he also began working on inventions and science experiments.

Narrator 1: In 1752, he conducted a famous experiment with electricity.

William Franklin: : Where are you going with that kite, father?

Ben: I am going to the field to test an idea I have about electricity.

William: But a storm is coming!

Ben: That's just what I am hoping. I believe that lightning conducts electricity. I have tied a metal key to the end of this kite. If lightning strikes the kite, it should travel down the string . . .

William: I see! The electric charge will make the metal key spark. Let me help you.

Narrator 2: Ben and his son William tried the experiment.

Narrator 1: Lightning struck the kite. The metal key sizzled with electricity, just as Ben guessed it would.

Narrator 2: It was a dangerous experiment, but an important one in the history of electricity.

SCENE 3: Ben Franklin the Statesman

Narrator 1: While he was conducting his experiments, Ben Franklin was also worried about his country.

Narrator 2: People in the American colonies did not feel they were treated fairly by the English government. They had to pay taxes to England, but they had no say in how the government was run.

Deborah: Where are you going, husband?

Ben: I am going to England, to talk to the king. He must understand that the people of the colonies should not have to pay these unfair taxes.

Narrator 1: Ben stayed in England from 1757 until 1762. He represented the people of the colonies. But things did not get better.

Narrator 2: War broke out in 1775 between the colonists and the British.

Narrator 1: In 1776, the colonists declared themselves independent from England. Ben Franklin was one of five men asked to write a Declaration of Independence.

Thomas Jefferson: I wrote the first draft. Ben Franklin changed some parts of it. We didn't let old Ben write the whole thing because he would have included too many jokes.

Narrator 2: Thomas Jefferson was just teasing, of course. Helping to write the Declaration of Independence was one of the most important things Ben Franklin ever did.

Narrator 1: Ben Franklin never stopped thinking, and inventing, and trying to make things better.

Narrator 2: In 1790 Franklin asked the United States government to make slavery against the law. He died two months later.

Narrator 1: Ben Franklin was busy to the end of his days.

Ben: As I always say, do not squander time, for that's the stuff life is made of!

The End

Busy Ben Franklin

Background

This play just touches on a few of the many accomplishments of Ben Franklin. Between his birth in 1706 and his death at age 84, he published the *Philadelphia Gazette* and *Poor Richard's Almanac*, which expressed his sense of humor; invented the Franklin stove, bifocals, the lightning rod, and a melodious instrument called the glass armonica; founded the first circulating library; founded a fire department and post office in Philadelphia; and was a key figure in the American Revolution and the foundation of democracy in the United States.

Note: Remember to point out to students that Franklin's lightning experiment is highly dangerous and should not be repeated.

Activity: Newspaper Fun

Ben Franklin was one of the first publishers to use cartoons, illustrations, and letters to the editor in his newspaper. With students, spend some time looking over these features in your local newspaper. Then invite students to create one of the following:

★ a cartoon that makes a comment about a story in the news

★ an illustration to accompany a news story they have read

★ a letter to the editor expressing their opinion on an issue in the news

Writing Prompt

Imagine that you had to study one of Benjamin Franklin's professions: printer, scientist, or statesman. Write a paragraph explaining which you would choose and why.

Discussion Question

Before you read this play, what did you know about Benjamin Franklin? Did you learn anything new?

Links

 Ben Franklin and the Magic Squares by Frank Murphy (Random House, 2001)

 The Electric Ben Franklin
www.ushistory.org/franklin/

Key Vocabulary

colonies: England set up thirteen colonies, or settlements, in North America

squander: waste

statesman: a person who is involved with government

The Truth About George Washington

by Tracey West

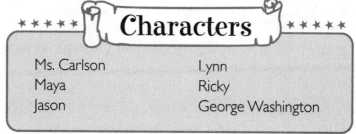

Characters

Ms. Carlson	Lynn
Maya	Ricky
Jason	George Washington

Ms. Carlson: Good morning, class. We are celebrating Presidents' Day today. Which group would like to read their report first?

Maya, Jason, Lynn, and Ricky: We would!

Ms. Carlson: Wonderful! I can't wait to hear about the president you chose.

Maya: We wrote about George Washington, the first president of the United States.

Jason: I drew a picture of him. *(Jason holds up a picture.)*

Lynn: George Washington was born on February 22, 1732, in Virginia. He practiced his spelling and handwriting in school. His favorite subject was math. He was a very good student.

Ricky: He was also very honest. When he was a boy, he chopped down a cherry tree. His father was very upset. He asked George if he did it, and George Washington said, "Yes. I cannot tell a lie."

George Washington: Excuse me, young man, but I believe you have made a mistake.

Maya: The picture! It's talking!

Washington: I'm sorry to interrupt you. But I have heard that cherry tree story many times, and it is just not true. It was made up by the man who wrote a biography of my life. He could have learned a thing or two about honesty, if you ask me.

Ricky: Sorry about that, Mr. Washington. We thought it was a true story. Would you like to hear the rest of our report?

Washington: I would like that. I will try not to interrupt again.

Ricky: George Washington was very strong. He liked to ride horses and play sports.

Maya: George Washington was so strong that he once threw a silver dollar all the way across the Potomac River.

Washington: Oh, dear.

Ms. Carlson: I can help, Mr. Washington. Maya, I think that story is just a myth too. It didn't really happen.

Washington: Of course it didn't. The Potomac River is over a mile wide! I was strong, but nobody could do that.

Maya: There are more facts in our report, Mr. Washington. Can we keep going?

Washington: By all means. This is very interesting.

Lynn: George Washington ran a plantation in Virginia. He also became a great soldier. He fought in the French and Indian War from 1755 to 1758.

Jason: And in 1775, when the American colonists went to war against England, George Washington became commander in chief of the Revolutionary Army.

Washington: Excellent! That is all correct. You children are very bright.

Ricky: After the war, George Washington helped to create a democracy in this country. He ran for president in 1789. He won the election and became the first president of the United States.

Washington: I'm sorry to do this again, but—

Ricky: Did we get something wrong?

Washington: I'm afraid so. You see, I didn't actually run for president.

Ms. Carlson: Now I'm confused. How did you become president if you didn't run?

Washington: After the war, the colonists wanted to make me king. I didn't want that at all. I wanted to live in a land where people could be free to choose their leaders and make their own decisions.

Maya: So that's why you helped set up a democracy.

Washington: Exactly. The first election for president was held in February 1789. But I had promised not to seek office. I did not campaign. I did not even ask for the job. But all of the states voted for me anyway.

Lynn: I guess you decided to take the job.

Washington: That's right. I could not turn my back on my country. It was a great honor to serve as president.

Ricky: We thought you were a great president. That's why we chose you for our report.

Washington: Thank you!

Jason: Speaking of our report, can we finish?

Washington: Please do.

Jason: George Washington was president from 1789 until 1797. When he got old, he wore false teeth made of wood.

Ms. Carlson: Let me help you out here, Mr. Washington. I know that this is just a myth too, right?

Washington: Correct. I did wear false teeth. But they were not made of wood.

Maya: I'm sorry we got so many things wrong, Mr. Washington.

Washington: That is quite all right. It has been more than 200 years since I was president. It can't be easy to keep the facts straight for all that time.

Ms. Carlson: Thank you for helping us, sir. You may sit down, group.

Jason: Ms. Carlson, may I draw another picture?

Ms. Carlson: Why, Jason?

Jason: I thought I'd find out if Abraham Lincoln has anything interesting to say!

The End

The Truth About George Washington

Background

Many of us have grown up hearing the same myths about George Washington: He chopped down a cherry tree; he wore wooden false teeth. This play clears up the facts about this key figure in history, who lived from 1732 to 1799 and served as our country's first president from 1789 to 1797.

Before reading the play, you may wish to ask students to tell anything they know about George Washington. If any myths are mentioned, write them on the chalkboard. Then return to them after reading and discuss with students what they've learned.

Activity: Fact Tree

The story of George Washington and the cherry tree may be a myth, but you can correct that error by creating a classroom tree full of facts about George Washington. On a bulletin board or large piece of poster paper, draw a tree trunk with branches. Cut out red "cherry" circles and give one to each student. Ask students to write one fact they know about George Washington, from the play or other classroom materials they have used. Hang the "fact cherries" from the tree. How many different facts was your class able to collect?

Writing Prompt

Imagine that you had the chance to talk to George Washington. Write down three questions you would ask him.

Discussion Question

What are some ways that people who study history can find out what is true and what is made up? *(They look at documents from the past, including letters and journals.)*

Links

 George Washington's Breakfast by Jean Fritz (Putnam & Grosset, 1998)

 Mount Vernon
www.mountvernon.org

Key Vocabulary

campaign: a plan that a candidate follows in order to win an election

democracy: a way of governing a country that allows people to elect officials

myth: a false idea that people believe

Betsy Ross
and the American Flag

by Katherine Noll

Characters

Narrator 1   Betsy Ross
Narrator 2   General George Washington
Uncle George   Robert Morris

SCENE 1

Narrator 1: Elizabeth Ross was born in Philadelphia, Pennsylvania, in 1752. Her friends called her Betsy.

Narrator 2: Betsy lived in difficult times. Pennsylvania was one of thirteen American colonies that were under the rule of Britain.

Narrator 1: The colonists living in America did not want to be ruled by Britain. They wanted to make their own rules and have their own government.

Narrator 2: In 1775, fighting began between British armies and American rebels. The American Revolution had begun.

Narrator 1: Betsy Ross and her husband John owned an upholstery business in Philadelphia. In colonial times, upholsterers did many different kinds of sewing.

Narrator 2: In early January of 1776, Betsy's husband was killed in the war.

Uncle George: I am so sorry, Betsy. John was a good nephew. Are you going to keep your business?

Betsy Ross: I am. The only thing I will stop doing is making furniture. John and I used to do that together. I will still sew curtains and other household items. But business is slow because of the war.

Uncle George: General Washington is doing an excellent job.

Betsy: I know he has been busy. I haven't seen him in church lately.

Uncle George: That's right. Your pew is right next to his, isn't it?

Betsy: Yes, it is. I wish I could help him.

Uncle George: Maybe we all can, Betsy. If we all work hard and stand together against the British, we will win.

SCENE 2

Narrator 1: Betsy kept working as a seamstress. Her shop was located in the back parlor of her home.

Narrator 2: Business was still slow. Fabric was hard to get because of the war.

Narrator 1: Even so, Betsy managed to keep her business going.

Narrator 2: One day in May 1776, Betsy got a knock on her door.

Betsy: Uncle George! How are you?

Uncle George: I am fine, Betsy. I hope you don't mind, but I brought some friends. This is Mr. Robert Morris, a businessman who is helping us raise money for our army. I believe you know General Washington.

Betsy: Yes, of course. Please come in.

General Washington: I need your help, Mrs. Ross. The American colonies will officially declare their independence from Britain in a few months. We need a flag for our new nation.

Uncle George: The flag is very important. We want it to stand for our freedom and independence.

General Washington: I also want the flag to bring our thirteen colonies together. Here is a sketch I made.

Betsy: I like it, but there is one thing I would change.

General Washington: What's that?

Betsy: These stars have six points. I think five-pointed stars would be nicer.

Robert Morris: Isn't that too difficult?

Betsy: No. I can cut a five-pointed star with a single snip of the scissors.

Narrator 1: Betsy went and got a piece of fabric.

Narrator 2: She folded the fabric a few times and . . .

Narrator 1: . . . with one quick snip from her scissor, she made a perfect five-point star!

General Washington: Very good! I think we should use this star for our flag. And I know we have found the woman for the job. What do you say, Mrs. Ross?

Betsy: It would be an honor.

SCENE 3

Narrator 2: Betsy talked it over with General Washington. Then she made a sketch of what the flag should look like.

Narrator 1: She sewed and stitched. In the end, she had a flag with thirteen red and white stripes. Thirteen stars, in a circle, rested on a blue field in the left-hand corner.

Narrator 2: The thirteen stars represented the thirteen colonies: Connecticut, Delaware, Georgia, Maryland, Massachusetts, New Hampshire, New Jersey, New York, North Carolina, Pennsylvania, Rhode Island, South Carolina, and Virginia.

Betsy: Here it is, General. I hope you like it.

**General
Washington:** It is beautiful. This is a flag of freedom. When it flies, it will inspire all of our soldiers. Thank you.

Betsy: I am glad I could help.

Narrator 1: One month later, the Declaration of Independence was written. The colonies were now their own country.

Narrator 2: A year later, on June 14, 1777, Betsy's flag was officially named the national flag.

Narrator 1: The American Revolution ended on September 3, 1783. Betsy's flag did not fly over the colonies of Britain anymore. The flag flew proudly over the United States of America, as it still does to this very day.

The End

Betsy Ross
and the American Flag

Background

Betsy Ross (1752–1836) was born Elizabeth Griscom. She married John Ross and together they ran a successful upholstering business. Betsy also made and repaired clothing. It is said that before George Washington ever approached her about making the American flag, Betsy had mended shirts for him.

The American Revolution began in 1775. The war years were very difficult for Betsy. Betsy lost two husbands to the war. British soldiers forcibly occupied Betsy's home during the winter of 1777. It was a struggle for Betsy to run her business during this time, but due to her efforts the business survived.

There is much debate as to whether Betsy Ross really did sew the first American flag. Although there is no written record of it, there are other facts that do support Ross having sewn the flag. Whatever the truth is, Betsy Ross was a remarkable, hardworking woman who survived the hardships of war.

Activity: Classroom Flag

George Washington wanted the American flag to unite the thirteen colonies. Ask your students what should be on a flag that would represent their classroom. Should there be a star for each student on the flag? What colors would be best? After deciding on what should go on the flag, create it. Using posterboard, paints, or crayons, make your classroom flag. The finished flag can be hung with pride where everyone can see it.

Writing Prompt

George Washington wanted his soldiers to feel proud when they saw the American flag. Write a paragraph describing how you feel when you see the American flag.

Discussion Question

The first flag had thirteen stars on it. Why does our flag today have 50 stars? *(to represent the 50 states)*

Links

 Betsy Ross by Alexandra Wallner (Holiday House, 1998)

 The Betsy Ross Homepage **www.ushistory.org/betsy/ index.html**

Key Vocabulary

independence: freedom

pew: a bench in a church

29

Sacagawea's Golden Dollar

by Katherine Noll

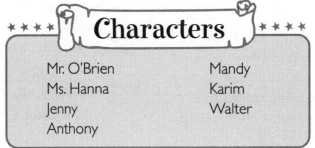

Characters

Mr. O'Brien	Mandy
Ms. Hanna	Karim
Jenny	Walter
Anthony	

Mr. O'Brien: Okay, class, quiet down! Our tour guide, Ms. Hanna, would like to begin.

Ms. Hanna: Thank you all for coming to the United States Mint in Philadelphia, Pennsylvania. Here at the Mint we make coins. A coin is a piece of money made from metal. Can anyone name a coin used for money?

Jenny: A penny?

Ms. Hanna: Correct! A penny is a coin used for money. It is worth one cent.

Anthony: How about a quarter?

Ms. Hanna: Good! A quarter is worth twenty-five cents.

Mandy: And a dollar!

Karim: A dollar is not a coin! It's made out of paper.

Mr. O'Brien: It doesn't have to be. What is Ms. Hanna holding in her hand?

Walter: It looks like a gold coin.

Ms. Hanna: Yes, this is the new golden dollar.

Karim: Wow! Is there a picture on it?

Jenny: I know Abraham Lincoln's picture is on the penny.

Anthony: And George Washington is on the quarter.

Karim: But who is on the golden dollar?

Ms. Hanna: Her name is Sacagawea (sa-CA-ga-WE-uh). I'll pass the coin around so everyone can see.

Walter: Sacagawea? Who is she? Why is she on the golden dollar?

Mr. O'Brien: Does anyone know who Sacagawea was?

Mandy: Wasn't Sacagawea a Native American woman?

Ms. Hanna: Very good. Sacagawea was a member of the Shoshone (sho-SHO-nee) tribe. She played a big part in the Lewis and Clark expedition.

Mr. O'Brien: We have just begun learning about this in class. In 1803, Thomas Jefferson was president. He wanted to send a group of people out West.

Ms. Hanna: The western part of the United States was unexplored. The only thing known about the West was that Native Americans lived there. Thomas Jefferson chose Meriwether Lewis and William Clark to lead the expedition. They had to explore the West and keep a journal of everything they saw. Lewis and Clark also had to make a map of the land.

Jenny: What does that have to do with Sacagawea?

Mr. O'Brien: Lewis and Clark were worried about traveling through the Native Americans' land. They did not know how strangers would be treated.

Ms. Hanna: Lewis and Clark hired Toussaint Charbonneau (too-SAUN shar-bone-OH), a French Canadian fur trader. Charbonneau's wife, Sacagawea, spoke two Native American languages, Shoshone and Hidatsa (i-DAT-sah).

Karim: I get it! They would need Sacagawea to translate for them.

Ms. Hanna: Yes. But Sacagawea ended up doing much more than that. In fact, during the long, hard trip Sacagawea had a baby boy.

Walter: So that's why there is a baby on her back in the picture on the coin.

Ms. Hanna: Even though she had a newborn baby to care for, Sacagawea still helped. She was able to guide the group through some of the most rugged wilderness.

Anthony: Didn't she also help out by finding food?

Mr. O'Brien: She knew how to find edible plants and roots.

Mandy: I know another way Sacagawea helped out. During one part of the trip, she rescued William Clark's journals. Their boat had turned over in the water, but Sacagawea stayed calm. She managed to save the journals.

Ms. Hanna: Sacagawea made the entire trip possible. Because the group traveled with a woman and a baby, the Native Americans knew they were peaceful. Not once were they attacked.

Mr. O'Brien: Sacagawea did more than just translate. She helped the expedition by getting some of the Native American tribes they encountered to sell the group horses. She also helped convince some Native Americans to guide the group.

Karim: She did all that? No wonder she was chosen for the golden dollar.

Anthony: How did they decide whom to put on the dollar?

Ms. Hanna: The U.S. Mint asked the public. We received letters, faxes, and e-mails. We also had public hearings.

Walter: Where did the Mint get the picture of Sacagawea?

Ms. Hanna: Different artists gave us pictures. The public voted on their favorite one.

Jenny: It's a beautiful picture. I like that the coin shows her baby on her back.

Ms. Hanna: Turn the coin over. Can anyone tell me what kind of bird is on the other side?

Mandy: It's an eagle!

Ms. Hanna: Yes, it is a flying bald eagle, which is a symbol of America. There are seventeen stars around the eagle. Does anyone know why?

Mr. O'Brien: That's a tough question.

Ms. Hanna: America had seventeen states at the time of the Lewis and Clark expedition. These stars each represent a state.

Karim: I never even knew there was a golden dollar coin.

Ms. Hanna: Now you do. The next time you see one, you can think of Sacagawea.

Jenny: And remember all the great things she did!

The End

Sacagawea's Golden Dollar

Background

The daughter of a Shoshone chief, Sacagawea was kidnapped by the Hidatsa Tribe when she was about ten years old. Sacagawea was sold to Toussaint Charbonneau and married to him.

Meriwether Lewis and William Clark set out to explore the West in 1803. Sacagawea's husband, Charbonneau, was hired as an interpreter, but Lewis and Clark were more interested in Sacagawea. A woman traveling with a party of men was considered a token of peace. Sacagawea's role turned out to be much larger than that of a mere peacekeeper. Her knowledge of the land and ability to find food proved invaluable.

Six years after the trip, Sacagawea had a daughter. No one is certain what happened to Sacagawea after that. It is believed she died in 1812.

Activity: A Dollar in Change

Divide the class into groups of four for this fun math game.

Materials:

✸ For each group: three dice

✸ For each player: 15 pennies, 10 nickels, 5 dimes, and 2 quarters (real or fake)

Directions:

1. For the first round, each player rolls one die. The player should put coins into the "pot" in the center of the table to equal the numerical value on the die. (For example: a student who rolls a three puts three pennies in the pot; a student who rolls a six could put in six pennies or one nickel and one penny.)

2. For the second round, each player rolls two dice instead of one.

3. For the third round, players roll all three dice.

4. Play continues with players rolling one, then two, then three dice. Keep going until there is a dollar's worth of change in the pot. The first player to roll and tip the total over one dollar wins the game.

Note: Advanced players can make change using the coins in the pot. Otherwise, players who don't have exact change to make a move must skip a turn.

Writing Prompt

Is there anyone you know who deserves to be on a coin? Write a letter to the U.S. Mint nominating this person. Give reasons why they should be on a coin.

Discussion Question

Do you think Sacagawea was a good choice for the golden dollar coin? Why or why not?

Links

 Picture Book of Sacagawea by David A. Adler (Holiday House, 2000)

 The United States Mint: The Life of Sacagawea

http://www.usmint.gov/mint_programs/ golden_dollar_coin/index.cfm?action= About_sacagawea

Key Vocabulary

edible: safe to eat

mint: a place where coins are made

The Ballad of Abraham Lincoln

by Tracey West

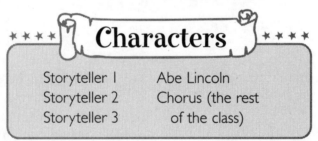

Characters

Storyteller 1	Abe Lincoln
Storyteller 2	Chorus (the rest
Storyteller 3	of the class)

VERSE 1

Storyteller 1: Come listen to the story of Abraham Lincoln.

Storyteller 2: By the time it's done, it'll have you thinking about the man they called Honest Abe.

Chorus: Abraham Lincoln.

VERSE 2

Storyteller 1: Abe was born in a log cabin in 1809.

Storyteller 2: His family lived in Kentucky, then crossed the state line.

Storyteller 3: They moved to Indiana when he was seven.

Chorus: Abe crossed the Kentucky line.

VERSE 3

Storyteller 1: Abe worked the family farm; he planted every seed.

Storyteller 2: But his favorite thing to do was find a book and read.

Storyteller 3: He read every chance he got.

Chorus: Abe Lincoln loved to read.

VERSE 4

Storyteller 1: Young Abe grew till he could grow no more.

Storyteller 2: He finally finished growing at six feet four.

Abe Lincoln: I was so tall I could barely fit through the door!

Chorus: Abe Lincoln was six foot four.

VERSE 5

Storyteller 1: Abe Lincoln moved to Illinois and quickly went to work.

Storyteller 2: He split logs, sorted mail, and worked as a store clerk.

Abe Lincoln: I finally decided to practice law.

Chorus: Abe Lincoln went to work.

VERSE 6

Storyteller 1: In Illinois Abe met a girl named Mary.

Storyteller 2: He knew she was the girl he was bound to marry.

Storyteller 3: So Mary Todd became Mary Lincoln.

Chorus: Abe Lincoln married Mary.

VERSE 7

Storyteller 1: After his marriage, Abe got involved in politics.

Storyteller 2: He was elected to Congress in 1846.

Abe Lincoln: We moved to Washington, D.C.

Chorus: Abe got involved in politics.

VERSE 8

Storyteller 1: Abe Lincoln moved on to do something great.

Storyteller 2: He was elected President of the United States.

Storyteller 3: November 6, 1860.

Chorus: He was elected President of the United States.

VERSE 9

Storyteller 1: One month later the country went to war.

Storyteller 2: The South didn't want to be part of the Union anymore.

Storyteller 3: They called themselves the Confederacy.

Chorus: And the country went to war.

VERSE 10

Storyteller 1:   The Confederates wanted the right to break free,

Storyteller 2:   to make their own laws, and to allow slavery.

Storyteller 3:   President Lincoln led the Union.

Chorus: But the Confederates wanted to break free.

VERSE 11

Storyteller 1:   President Lincoln signed a law in 1863.

Storyteller 2:   He signed a law to abolish slavery.

Abe Lincoln: I signed the Emancipation Proclamation.

Chorus: It abolished slavery.

VERSE 12

Storyteller 1:   By 1865, the Civil War was done.

Storyteller 2:   The Confederates surrendered and the Union had won.

Storyteller 3:   Celebrations broke out in Washington.

Chorus: The Civil War was done.

VERSE 13

Storyteller 1:   Just days later, Abe went out with his wife.

Storyteller 2:   While sitting in Ford's Theater, a gunshot took his life.

Storyteller 3:   John Wilkes Booth shot the President.

Chorus: Abe Lincoln lost his life.

VERSE 14

Storyteller 1:   That's the end of the story of Abraham Lincoln.

Storyteller 2:   We hope it's a story that's got you thinking.

Storyteller 3:   The world won't forget Honest Abe.

Chorus: We won't forget Abraham Lincoln.

The End

The Ballad of Abraham Lincoln

Background

This play presents, in the rhyming stanzas of a ballad, the milestones in the life of Abraham Lincoln. One of the reasons Lincoln has remained popular in the minds of Americans is the story of his humble beginnings. Born in a log cabin in Kentucky, Lincoln survived the death of his mother at age nine and the harsh conditions of living on the frontier. He went to school only sporadically, and largely educated himself.

Lincoln is also remembered as a leader who shepherded the country through the difficult times of the Civil War. While his signing of the Emancipation Proclamation is a key moment in our country's history, in recent years scholars have questioned his racial views. Lincoln himself stated that he did not believe in equality between black and white races. Even so, the fact that he protected the Union, freed the slaves, and died tragically at the peak of his life have ensured him an honored place in American history.

Activity: Class Picture Book

Using the ballad as a starting point, work with the class to write on the chalkboard one-line facts about Abraham Lincoln. Try to come up with as many facts as there are students in the class. When you are done, assign one line to each student. Have students copy their fact on the bottom of a plain piece of white paper. On the top of the page, have students illustrate the fact.

When all of the pages are finished, staple them together to make a class picture book about Abraham Lincoln. As a class, decide on a title for the book. (If there weren't enough facts to go around, some students could be assigned to create the front and back covers.) Keep the book available at a reading center for students to enjoy on their own.

Writing Prompt

Write a four-line verse describing an important event in your life. (Encourage students to repeat the rhyme scheme in this ballad, or come up with one of their own.)

Discussion Question

What did you learn about Abraham Lincoln by reading this ballad?

Links

 A. Lincoln and Me by Louise Borden (Scholastic, 2001)

 <u>Abraham Lincoln</u>
www.whitehouse.gov/history/ presidents/al16.html

Key Vocabulary

abolish: to put an end to something officially

emancipation: the act of freeing a person or group from slavery

Confederacy: the group of 11 states that declared itself independent from the rest of the United States just before the Civil War

Union: the United States of America

Aunt Harriet's Story

by Katherine Noll

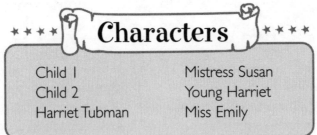

Characters

Child 1	Mistress Susan
Child 2	Young Harriet
Harriet Tubman	Miss Emily

SCENE 1

Child 1: Aunt Harriet, please tell us a story!

Child 2: What was it like to be a slave? Were you afraid to run away?

Child 1: I want to hear how you escaped from the plantation. What did it feel like when you were finally free?

Harriet Tubman: So many questions! I was afraid to run away. But I was more afraid to live my life as a slave. Everyone, come sit down. I'll tell you a story about when I was little.

Child 2: Where did you live, Aunt Harriet?

Harriet Tubman: I was born in Maryland. Maryland is a southern state. In Maryland, like many other southern states, it was legal to own slaves. I lived on a big farm, or a plantation. I had to work out in the hot sun all day long. One day I was outside when this woman came and took me away . . . .

SCENE 2

Mistress Susan: Girl, you come along with me. Hop in the wagon.

Young Harriet: Yes, ma'am.

Mistress Susan: I made arrangements with your master. You will come and live with me. I need someone to clean my house and take care of my baby. I hope you can do a good job.

Young Harriet: Yes, ma'am.

Harriet Tubman: This woman had hired me to work at her house. But all the money I made went to the master of the plantation, who owned the farm and all the slaves on it.

Mistress Susan: Now as soon as we get home I want you to clean and dust the parlor.

Harriet Tubman: I had worked inside a house only a few times before. I always liked to be outside. I had never dusted before.

Young Harriet: I swept and dusted, ma'am.

Mistress Susan: You lazy girl! Look at this room. It's still filthy!

Harriet Tubman: I looked around the room. I couldn't believe my eyes! All the dust and dirt I had just cleaned were still there.

Mistress Susan: Come with me.

Harriet Tubman: That woman whipped me for not cleaning the room right.

Child 1: Aunt Harriet, how terrible!

Harriet Tubman: It got worse. Every day I swept and dusted, and every day the dust settled back down. And every day I was whipped. I could not understand what I was doing wrong.

Mistress Susan: I've had enough of you! Come with me, you will get your punishment.

Miss Emily: What is going on, sister? What is all the fuss about?

Mistress Susan: This lazy girl can't clean the parlor. I'm punishing her.

Miss Emily: Maybe she never learned how. Leave her with me, I'll show her.

Harriet Tubman: Susan's sister, Emily, showed me what I was doing wrong. I had to open all the windows first, so the dust had somewhere to go. Then I had to sweep *before* I dusted the furniture. If someone had shown me from the start how to do it, I would have been able to do it right. But Mistress Susan was a mean woman, and because I was a slave, there was nothing I could do about it.

SCENE 3

Mistress Susan: Hurry up, Harriet. I need you to clean the kitchen and wash the dishes before bed.

Young Harriet: Yes, ma'am.

Harriet Tubman: If only I could have gone to sleep! Instead, I spent the night sitting next to Mistress Susan's bed, by her baby's cradle. I had to rock the cradle all night long. Mistress Susan slept with a small whip next to the bed. If I fell asleep and the baby started crying, she would whip my neck and shoulders.

Young Harriet: Hush, little baby, don't say a word . . .

Harriet Tubman: I couldn't help but fall asleep! I was tired from working all day. And when I slept, I could dream I was with my mother and father in our cabin. I missed them so much.

Mistress Susan: The baby is crying! What have I told you, you lazy girl?

Harriet Tubman: It didn't matter if I said I was sorry, or if I told her I was tired. I would get whipped no matter what.

Child 1: Is that how you got those scars on your neck?

Harriet Tubman: Yes, it is.

SCENE 4

Child 2: How did you survive? That's a terrible way to live.

Harriet Tubman: When all those terrible things happened, I knew one day I would be free. I could not live a life in slavery. I knew I would risk anything to escape to the North.

Child 1: But once you escaped, you didn't stay in the North. You kept coming back to the South to save other slaves.

Child 2: That's right. You helped slaves escape on the Underground Railroad. Was the Underground Railroad a train that ran underground?

Harriet Tubman: No. The Underground Railroad was a secret group of people and places used by slaves to get to the North.

Child 1:   Were you scared to go back to the South?

Harriet Tubman: I knew I wouldn't be happy until every slave was free. The worst part of slavery was how families were torn apart. My sisters were sold away to the deep South. Mothers and children were sold away from each other. No person should have to live such a life. I was so happy every time I could help free another slave.

Child 2:   You are very brave, Aunt Harriet.

Harriet Tubman: Thank you, but I only did what I could.

Child 1:   Now tell us a story about the Underground Railroad!

Harriet Tubman: Maybe tomorrow!

The End

Aunt Harriet's Story

Background

In 1820, Harriet Tubman was born a slave on a plantation in Maryland. From a very young age, Harriet worked as a field hand, a cook, a maid, and a woodcutter.

As a slave, Harriet was beaten regularly. While she was trying to help a runaway slave, an overseer struck Harriet in the head with a lead weight. She was in a coma for several months. For the rest of her life, Harriet suffered blackouts due to this injury. In spite of this handicap, Harriet not only managed to escape to freedom, but she helped over three hundred others flee a life of slavery too.

During the Civil War, Harriet Tubman served as a spy and a nurse for the Union army. When the war was over, she settled in Auburn, New York. She established a home for orphans and the elderly. She died there on March 10, 1913.

Activity: A Difficult Decision

Divide a large piece of paper or posterboard in half. Ask students to name the benefits of escaping from slavery. (Examples: *You would not have a master. No one could sell you away from your family. You would be paid for your hard work.*) Write their answers on the left side of the chart. Then ask students to name things that might be difficult about trying to escape from slavery. (Examples: *You would be punished, maybe even killed, if you were caught. You might have to leave family behind. You would be going to a strange place where you might not know anyone.*) Write these answers on the right side of the chart. Then ask the class to look at the chart and think about Harriet Tubman's decision to run away, and to help others escape. What does this say about her character?

Writing Prompt

Write a paragraph summarizing the story that Harriet Tubman tells in the play.

Discussion Question

This play shows the horrible treatment Harriet Tubman suffered through as a slave. How did you feel when you read the play? What would you have done if you were living in those times? Would you have tried to help slaves escape even though it was dangerous?

Links

Minty: A Story of Young Harriet Tubman by Alan Schroeder (Dial Books for Young Readers, 1996)

Harriet Tubman and the Underground Railroad
http://www2.lhric.org/pocantico/tubman /tubman.html

Key Vocabulary

plantation: a large farm in a warm climate where crops such as coffee and cotton are grown

Clara Barton
Angel of the Battlefield

by Katherine Noll

Characters

Narrator 1	Elizabeth (Clara's friend)
Clara Barton	Soldier 1
Sarah Barton	Soldier 2
Stephen Barton	Dr. Joseph K. Barnes, U.S. Surgeon General
Narrator 2	Duchess of Baden

SCENE 1

Narrator 1: Clara Barton was born on Christmas Day, 1821, in Oxford, Massachusetts. Clara was a quiet farm girl. But she always wanted to help other people.

Clara Barton: Mother, what's the matter?

Sarah Barton:	Your brother David was hurt very badly. He fell from the roof of the barn.
Clara:	Oh, no! Will he be all right?
Sarah:	Yes, he will. But he will need someone to nurse him day and night.
Clara:	I can do it!
Sarah:	I don't know, Clara. You are only eleven years old. It's a big job.
Clara:	Please, Mother. Let me do it. I know I can take good care of him.
Sarah:	It will be hard, but if you really want to . . .
Clara:	Yes!
Narrator 1:	For two years, Clara nursed her brother. She learned much about nursing and helping people.

SCENE 2

Narrator 2:	As Clara grew older she continued to help people. She worked as a teacher. In 1861, she was living in Washington, D.C. The Civil War had started.
Elizabeth:	Clara, did you hear about those soldiers from Massachusetts?
Clara:	No. What happened?
Elizabeth:	They lost all their supplies in a battle. The soldiers have no clothing or food.
Clara:	How awful! We must do something.
Narrator 2:	Clara went right to work. She tore up old sheets for towels. She cooked for the troops.
Soldier 1:	Thank you, Miss Barton.

Soldier 2: What would we have done without you?

Narrator 1: Clara heard stories about the war. The soldiers did not have bandages and other medical supplies. Many soldiers did not even have enough to eat.

Clara: I have to help. But what can I do? I don't have enough food and supplies for an entire army.

Elizabeth: I want to help too. I'm sure many people feel the same way.

Clara: You're right! They just need to know how to help. I will take out an advertisement in the newspaper. I'll ask people to donate food and supplies for our soldiers.

Narrator 2: Clara had a smart idea. Many people donated items. Now Clara had to get to the troops in the battlefield to deliver the supplies.

Dr. Joseph Barnes: Miss Barton, I am happy to help you. As U.S. Surgeon General, I give you permission to travel anywhere, and into any battlefield, in order to help soldiers and give out supplies.

Clara: Thank you, Dr. Barnes. I will do my best to help.

Narrator 2: Clara went into the battlefields again and again. She helped the sick and injured. She also gave out bandages, clothes, and food. Because of her hard work and care, the soldiers called her the "Angel of the Battlefield."

SCENE 3

Narrator 1: After the Civil War, Clara was tired. She had seen many sad things. In 1869 she went to Geneva, Switzerland for a rest. But Clara couldn't rest for long. The Franco-Prussian War had begun in Europe.

Clara: Another war! More people will suffer. I have to help.

Duchess of Baden: We can volunteer for the Red Cross.

Clara: The Red Cross? What is that?

Duchess: The Red Cross gives out medicine and food to soldiers. They do many good things. It is like what you did for the soldiers in America.

Narrator 2: Clara stayed in Europe and helped. The German Emperor, William I, learned of her hard work and awarded her the Iron Cross of Merit. It was a great honor.

SCENE 4

Narrator 1: Clara returned home to America. She had an idea.

Clara: I want to start a branch of the Red Cross here in America. I wrote to the founder of the International Red Cross in Europe.

Elizabeth: And what did he say?

Clara: I am president of the new American Red Cross.

Elizabeth: Think of all the good you can do!

Clara: There is much to be done. The war is over. But people suffer every day.

Elizabeth: I know. I read in the newspaper this morning about floods in Ohio. Many families lost their homes.

Clara: Really? The Red Cross will be there.

Narrator 2: The Red Cross was there, and in many other places. People who were hurt by disasters such as fires, floods, and earthquakes could turn to the Red Cross for help. The Red Cross donated food and provisions. They also gave people who lost their homes a place to stay.

Narrator 1: Clara Barton was president of the American Red Cross until 1904. She was 82 years old when she resigned.

Narrator 2: There is a monument to Clara Barton at the Antietam (an-TEE-tum) National Battlefield. It reads:

CLARA BARTON
During the battle of Antietam
September 17, 1862
Clara Barton brought supplies
and nursing aid to the wounded
on this battlefield.
This act of love and mercy
led to the birth of the present
AMERICAN
NATIONAL RED CROSS.

Narrator 1: Because of Clara Barton, the American Red Cross is still helping people. Her good deeds will always be remembered.

The End

Clara Barton
Angel of the Battlefield

Background

During the Civil War, Clara Barton passed bravely through battle lines, handing out supplies, nursing the wounded, and searching for the missing. She became famous for her good works and was soon known as the "angel of the battlefield."

While resting in Europe after the war, the Franco-Prussian War broke out. (This was a war between France and several German states including Prussia, the largest state.) There Clara discovered the International Red Cross. This organization was founded in Geneva, Switzerland in 1863, with the goal of providing nonpartisan care to those sick or wounded in times of war.

Returning to America, Clara Barton organized the American Red Cross. She also expanded the Red Cross to provide relief in cases of natural disaster. Clara Barton remained president of the American Red Cross until she was 82 years old. She died eight years later on April 12, 1912.

Activity: Classroom First Aid Kit

Clara Barton helped the soldiers by giving them basic first aid. Make a first aid kit for your classroom. (Or make one and donate it to the school nurse.) Use a red plastic lunch box. Glue a piece of white paper to one side. Cut out a large red cross. Glue it in the middle of the paper. Write *First Aid* in large black letters on top of the cross. Ask students to donate supplies from home. Some suggestions are: adhesive bandages in assorted sizes, sterile gauze, antibiotic ointment, instant ice packs, plastic gloves, elastic bandages, and emergency phone numbers.

Writing Prompt

Have you ever helped someone in trouble, or has someone helped you? If so, write a paragraph about the situation and how it made you feel.

Discussion Question

You have probably seen the Red Cross on the television news, helping people recover from disasters such as floods, earthquakes, or the September 11 terrorist attacks. What kinds of things did the Red Cross do to help?

Links

 Clara Barton: Angel of the Battlefield by Rae Bains (Troll, 1982)

 The American Red Cross Museum **www.redcross.org/museum/**

Key Vocabulary

troops: organized groups of soldiers

volunteer: to work without pay

The Wright Flight

by Tracey West

★ ★ ★ ★ **Characters** ★ ★ ★ ★

Time Traveler Terry   Orville Wright

Time Traveler Tina   Wilbur Wright

Mr. Daniels

SCENE I

Time Traveler Terry: Time Traveler Terry here. Today Tina and I are traveling back in time to December 17, 1903.

Time Traveler Tina: For all you history buffs out there, we are here to see the Wright brothers' first airplane flight.

Terry: As you can see, we are standing on a sandy beach in Kitty Hawk, North Carolina. It is very windy and cold.

Tina: The Wright brothers and their guests are keeping warm inside a small camp house they have set up. I can see one of the guests leaving the house now. Let's see if we can get an interview.

Terry: Excuse me, but can you tell us why the Wright brothers chose such a cold, windy place for their flight?

Mr. Daniels: Well, the beach here is perfect for a test flight. The wind may help keep the plane in the air. And the soft, sandy ground is good for landing.

Terry: That makes sense.

Tina: Someone else is coming out of the house. It's Orville Wright!

Terry: Orville, who will be flying the plane today?

Orville: I will. My brother and I tossed a coin last Monday to see who would get to fly. My brother won, but the plane sank just after it lifted off. So today it's my turn.

Tina: Can you tell us what is so important about this flight today?

Orville: Certainly. You see, my brother and I have flown in a glider before. So have other aviators.

Terry: What's a glider?

Orville: A glider is like a plane. It has wings, and a place for a pilot to ride. But it has no motor, so it can only go as far as the wind carries it.

Tina: Can you control the way a glider moves?

Orville: My brother and I were the first to figure out a way to do that. But we think our plane will be even better.

Mr. Daniels: I'm sure you will succeed.

Orville: Thank you. Would you mind using my camera to photograph this event?

Mr. Daniels: I'd be happy to.

Orville: Now if you'll excuse me, I must get ready for the test flight.

Terry: Thanks, Orville!

SCENE 2

Tina: Wilbur Wright is now coming out of the camp house. Let's see if he'll talk to us.

Terry: Mr. Wright, can you tell me how you and your brother got the idea to build an airplane?

Wilbur: You could say that it all started with bicycles.

Terry: Bicycles?

Wilbur: Yes. My brother and I have always been interested in how things work. About ten years ago, we opened a bicycle repair shop. I was riding my bicycle one day when I realized that balance was the key to riding it. I thought balance might help a glider stay up in the air.

Tina: What did you do then?

Wilbur: I studied everything I could about flight. Orv and I began building kites and gliders a few years later. All of that hard work has led up to this moment.

Terry: Thanks, Mr. Wright. I can't wait to see what happens today!

SCENE 3

Tina: I can see the Wright Brothers' flyer from here. It's about forty feet wide from wing to wing.

Terry: Orville Wright is climbing onto the plane. He is lying face down on the body of the plane. He is holding onto the rudder controls, which he will use to steer the plane.

Tina: The brothers' guests are coming out of the camp house. It's time for the flight!

Terry: The motor has started. The plane's propellers are turning.

Tina: The plane is rising into the air! It's moving forward.

Terry: The flight looks bumpy. Orville is having a hard time keeping the plane in the air.

Tina: The plane has landed. The flight is over. Let's talk to the brothers.

Orville: We did it, Wilbur! How long was it?

Wilbur: You stayed in the air for twelve seconds.

Terry: Twelve seconds? What's the big deal about that?

Orville: It's a very big deal, young man. This is the first time in history that a plane was raised in the air by its own power.

Wilbur: It's also the first flight to carry a passenger in a forward direction without losing speed.

Orville: We've done what no one else has been able to do.

Mr. Daniels: I got it on film, Orville. What happens next?

Wilbur: It's too cold to stay out here. Let's warm up in the camp house and try another flight.

Tina: So there you have it, folks. You've just seen the first manned, powered, controlled flight in history.

Terry: That was twelve seconds I will never forget!

The End

The Wright Flight

Background

Before Wilbur and Orville Wright made their historic flight in 1903, other aviators had experimented with manned gliders. Although neither brother graduated from high school, they were both fascinated with how things work. They built their first glider in 1899.

The significance of the December 17 flight is threefold: It was powered by a motor, the pilot was able to control the movement of the plane, and flight was sustained—it sailed in a forward motion without reducing speed. The flyer's design was simple, but pivotal. The entire aerospace industry is founded on the pioneering work of the Wright brothers.

Activity: Paper in Flight

Have fun exploring aviation by making paper planes as a class. Use resources such as the Web site jline Paper Airplanes **www.freehomepages.com/jline** or *The Paper Airplane Book* by Seymour Simon (Viking, 1976) to create different kinds of planes.

When the planes are finished, conduct test flights. Ask students to predict how far their planes will go, and which kind of plane will go farthest. Keep a record of the test flights and chart the results.

Writing Prompt

Imagine you could travel back in time to witness the Wright brothers' first flight. Write a report describing what you see.

Discussion Question

Have you ever ridden on an airplane? How was your experience different from the Wright brothers' flight? How was it similar?

Links

 First Flight: The Story of Tom Tate and the Wright Brothers by George Shea (Scott Foresman, 1997)

Wright Again (The Franklin Institute Online) **www.fi.edu/wright/again.html**

Key Vocabulary

aviator: a person who builds or flies aircraft

rudder: a hinged plate attached to an airplane that is used for steering

George Washington Carver: Man of Ideas

by Katherine Noll

Characters

Farmer Jones	Narrator
Mrs. Jones	George Washington Carver
Daniel Jones	Theodore

SCENE 1

Farmer Jones: I can't believe it! None of the seeds I planted grew at all. All I have is dirt.

Mrs. Jones: What will we do? We need to grow and sell cotton. It is how we earn a living.

Farmer Jones: Something is wrong with the soil here. Other farmers have been having the same problem.

Mrs. Jones: I hope we can do something. If we don't, many people are going to go hungry.

Daniel Jones: Ma! Pa! Boll weevils have destroyed Mr. Jemison's cotton crop.

Farmer Jones: Things don't look good for our farms.

Narrator: In 1914 farmers in the South were in big trouble. Years of growing cotton had left the soil in poor shape. There were no nutrients in the soil to help grow healthy new plants. When farmers could grow cotton, many times it was attacked by boll weevils. Boll weevils are insects that feed on cotton plants.

SCENE 2

George Washington Carver: I need to find a way to help southern farmers.

Narrator: George Washington Carver was a scientist. He wanted to find a way to fix the problem the farmers were having.

George: The cotton has left the soil weak. I need to find a way to put nutrients back into the soil.

Theodore: But can it be done, Mr. Carver?

George: Here at Tuskegee (tusk-EE-gee) Institute, I have the tools to test my ideas. We even have our own farm to try out new ideas.

Theodore: What ideas do you have?

George: Right now, we are looking at peanuts, soybeans, and sweet potatoes. These plants give nutrients back to the soil as they grow.

Theodore: That's amazing!

George: If it works, we could save the farmers in the South.

SCENE 3

Mrs. Jones: What are you reading, dear?

Farmer Jones: A scientist named George Washington Carver thinks he can save our farm.

Daniel: Really? How?

Farmer Jones: He says we should plant peanuts instead of cotton.

Mrs. Jones: Peanuts? But we have always planted cotton.

Daniel: Who is this man?

Farmer Jones: He is an African-American scientist who works at the Tuskegee Institute. He says that tests have been done that prove peanuts will make our soil healthy again.

Mrs. Jones: What do you think? It's a big risk. I'm not sure we can make money selling peanuts.

Farmer Jones: We have to try it. I can't grow cotton anymore.

SCENE 4

Theodore: Farmers in the South have been growing peanuts, Mr. Carver.

George: Yes, and the soil is healthy again. But there is a problem.

Theodore: What?

George: The farmers are growing lots of peanuts. But nobody wants to buy the peanuts.

Theodore: What can you do about that? You are a scientist, not a salesman.

George: I can use science to sell peanuts. I will find different ways for people to use them.

Narrator: Peanut butter had been invented years before, but it wasn't popular yet. George wanted to find as many new ways as possible to use the peanut. He worked in his lab at the Tuskegee Institute in Alabama.

George: And this is a cheese made from peanuts.

Theodore: Cheese?

George: Yes, and this is peanut milk.

Theodore: Peanut milk? Wow!

George: There's much more where this came from.

Narrator: George Washington Carver developed more than three hundred products from peanuts.

SCENE 5

Farmer Jones: We grew a lot of peanuts this year, but we didn't sell many of them.

Daniel: Did you see the newspaper? George Washington Carver has come up with hundreds of uses for the peanut.

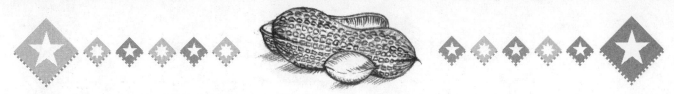

Mrs. Jones: Like what?

Daniel: It says here: Coffee, ink, medicine . . .

Farmer Jones: Let me see that! And soap, medicines, and dyes made
from peanuts!

Mrs. Jones: Do you think this will help us sell more peanuts?

Farmer Jones: I think it will.

SCENE 6

George: I've just learned that peanuts are the second biggest crop
in the South.

Theodore: The southern farms are able to plant many different crops now.
The soil is healthy again.

Narrator: George Washington Carver's efforts helped save southern farmers.
People from all over the world asked for his advice on farming.
Carver donated his life savings to the Tuskegee Institute.
He wanted people to keep learning and studying farming.

SCENE 7

Farmer Jones: We did it! We sold all our peanuts!

Mrs. Jones: The farm is saved. I wonder if George Washington Carver knows
how many people he has helped.

Daniel: If I ever met him, I would shake his hand and say thank you.

Farmer Jones: I would give him a barrel of peanuts!
Thank you, George Washington Carver.

The End

George Washington Carver: Man of Ideas

Background

George Washington Carver was born a slave in 1861. His mother disappeared after the Civil War was over, and his old slave master, Moses Carver, and his wife took George in and raised him. At age 12, George left the Carvers' to obtain an education. He studied in a one-room schoolhouse while he worked as a farmhand. Although he was denied admission to a university in Kansas because he was black, Carver was able to attend college in Iowa. At Iowa State Agricultural College he received degrees in agriculture and science.

George Washington Carver became director of the department of agriculture at the Tuskegee Institute. There Carver spent his time developing ways to help poor farmers. His experiments with the peanut ended the South's dependency on cotton for good. Carver was given job offers from many prominent people, including Thomas A. Edison. But he chose instead to spend his life at Tuskegee, devoting his time to his studies and experiments, until his death in 1943.

Activity: Peanut Products

Have students pretend they are going on a trip to the supermarket to buy products that contain peanuts. Ask them to write a list of what they will buy. Combine student lists to make one long class shopping list. How many different products did your class think of?

Writing Prompt

Imagine you are a scientist like George Washington Carver. Write a story about what you would invent. Would your invention help people? Or would you invent something just for fun?

Discussion Question

George Washington Carver was turned away from one college because he was African-American. How do you think life would be different for the farmers in the South if Carver never became a scientist?

Links

 A Weed is a Flower: The Life of George Washington Carver by Aliki (Aladdin Paperbacks, 1988)

 The Legacy of George Washington Carver
www.lib.iastate.edu/spcl/gwc/home.html

Key Vocabulary

boll weevils: insects that infect and eat cotton plants

nutrients: substances such as vitamins and minerals that keep plants, people, and animals healthy

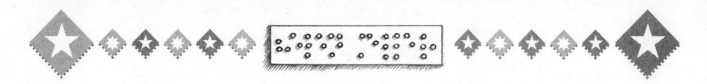

The Courage of Helen Keller

by Katherine Noll

★★★★ Characters ★★★★

Narrator 1	Doctor
Narrator 2	Susan (Kate's friend)
Kate Keller	Annie Sullivan
Captain Keller	

SCENE 1

Narrator 1: Captain Keller and his wife, Kate, stood next to the doctor as he examined their baby. The year was 1882, and the baby's name was Helen Keller.

Narrator 2: Helen had been very sick with scarlet fever. The fever was gone. But something still seemed wrong with Helen.

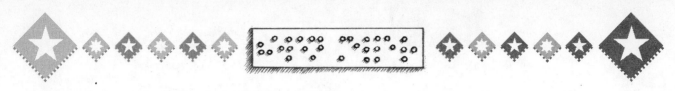

Kate Keller: Doctor, how is Helen?

**Captain
Keller:**   The fever is gone, but she is so quiet.

Doctor: I'm afraid I have very bad news for you. Helen's illness has left her blind and deaf.

Kate Keller: Do you mean she can't see or hear anything?

Doctor: Yes. I'm very sorry.

Narrator 1:   Helen's parents were very sad. Their little baby girl, not even two years old, was trapped in a world of darkness and silence. Helen could not hear their voices or see their faces.

Narrator 2:   If Helen was just deaf, her parents could teach her sign language. Sign language is a system of hand gestures that stand for words. But since Helen was also blind, she could not see the hand gestures.

Narrator 1:   The Kellers did not know how to talk to Helen. But they tried to help Helen and to make her happy.

Susan: It must be so hard for Helen. How does she get around?

Kate Keller: We spend a lot of time together. She holds onto my skirts as I walk around the house. Helen uses her sense of touch and smell to get around, and to learn about new things. Helen is a smart girl. She gets upset when we do not understand her.

Susan: Is she cold? She has wrapped her arms around herself and she is shivering!

Kate: No, she is just telling me she wants ice cream. (*to Helen*) No, Helen. Not now. Maybe after supper.

Narrator 2:   Helen put her hand on her mother's head. She felt her mother shaking her head from side to side.

Narrator 1:   Helen knew this meant no. She grew very angry. Picking up a glass vase, she hurled it at the floor.

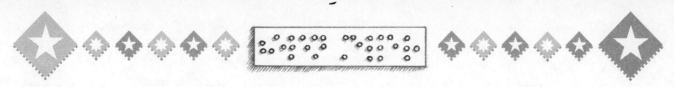

Susan: Oh my goodness! What are you going to do with this child?

Kate: I don't know.

SCENE 2

Narrator 2:   Helen felt angry. She knew that other people could talk with their mouths. But every time Helen tried to speak, nobody understood her. For Helen, the world was a confusing and scary place.

Narrator 1:   Her parents wanted Helen to be able to communicate. They also wanted her to stop having temper tantrums. So they hired a teacher named Annie Sullivan to work with Helen.

Captain Keller: I hope you can help us, Miss Sullivan. You are our last hope.

Annie Sullivan: I have learned some things at the Perkins School for the Blind that may help.

Kate Keller: Miss Sullivan, let me introduce you to Helen.

Annie Sullivan: Here Helen, I have a present for you. Some blind students at the Perkins Institute made this doll for you.

Narrator 2:   Annie placed the doll in Helen's hand. In her other hand, Annie used sign language to spell D-O-L-L. If Helen could not see sign language, Annie wanted to teach her how to feel it.

Kate: Let's sit down and have lunch. Miss Sullivan must be hungry after her long trip.

Narrator 1:   Everyone sat down for lunch. Instead of using a fork, Helen grabbed the food with her hands. Annie, surprised at this, made Helen pick up a fork. Helen threw the fork to the floor.

Annie Sullivan: If she won't eat with a fork, she won't eat at all.

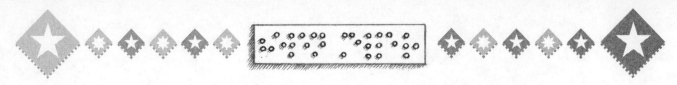

Kate: Miss Sullivan, don't you think you are being too hard on her?

Annie Sullivan: She has to learn the right way to do things. It won't be easy, and Helen may not like it, but it must be done.

SCENE 3

Narrator 2: Mr. and Mrs. Keller did not like to see Helen punished. Sometimes when Annie would punish Helen, her mother would come and stop the punishment. Annie was afraid Helen would never learn.

Narrator 1: The Kellers decided to let Annie and Helen stay in a small cottage near their house. Helen soon learned to behave, but would she ever learn to communicate?

Annie Sullivan: D-O-L-L. Like this.

Narrator 2: Annie spelled doll into Helen's hand.

Annie Sullivan: Now you try. Very good, Helen. You spelled it perfectly. But do you understand what it means?

Narrator 1: Helen could spell many words. But she still did not know that the words meant something. Helen could spell doll, but she did not know it meant the soft toy she was holding in her hand.

Annie Sullivan: Well, Helen, we've been at this for a month. You still don't understand. Let's go outside and keep practicing.

Narrator 2: Annie led Helen outside. They walked over to a water pump. Annie pumped water over Helen's hand. In the other hand, she spelled W-A-T-E-R using sign language.

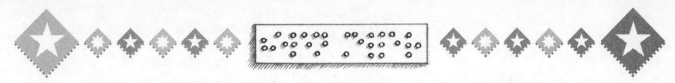

Narrator 1:   Annie spelled the word over and over again. Helen grew excited. She finally understood! The letters Annie kept spelling in her hand were names for real things!

Annie Sullivan: Helen, you know. Yes, this is water!

Narrator 2:   Helen grabbed Annie. Now that she finally understood, she wanted to know the names of everything.

Annie Sullivan: This is the earth. E-A-R-T-H. This is the cat. C-A-T. Oh, and this is grass. G-R-A-S-S.

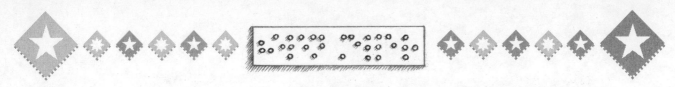

Narrator 1: Helen finally had a way to talk with other people. She could let people know what she was thinking and feeling. And Annie could now teach her how to read Braille, a system of raised dots that blind people feel in order to read.

Captain Keller: Thank you, Miss Sullivan. You are a great teacher.

Kate Keller: You have given my daughter a new life. Thank you.

Annie Sullivan: Helen is smart and determined. Because of her strength and courage, she did not give up. She kept trying to understand.

Narrator 2: Helen never stopped learning. She learned how to read and write Braille. She also learned how to speak with the help of speech teachers.

Narrator 1: Helen Keller graduated from college in 1904. After college, she devoted her life to helping people all over the world.

The End

The Courage of Helen Keller

Background

Helen Keller was born on June 27, 1880. At the age of 19 months she became very ill with what is believed to have been scarlet fever. Her illness left her blind, deaf, and mute.

An exceptionally smart child, Helen would suffer fits of rage when she could not communicate with her parents. The Kellers had her examined by Alexander Graham Bell when she was six years old. Bell arranged for Annie Sullivan, from the Perkins Institution for the Blind, to teach Helen.

Annie was successful. Once Helen could communicate, she was an eager student. She learned Braille, and eventually learned how to speak. Helen Keller graduated from college in 1904. She dedicated her life to helping blind and deaf people all over the world. Helen helped establish the American Foundation for the Blind. She died on June 1, 1968.

Activity: Braille Buddies

Hand out copies of the Braille alphabet. Explain that the dots and lines represent letters of the alphabet. Blind people can read Braille by feeling the raised, bumpy symbols with their fingers.

Instruct your students to pick three short words. (The words should have no more than three or four letters.) They must keep these words a secret! Have the students write the words in Braille. Divide the class into pairs. Have students switch papers with their partner. Now they must use the Braille alphabet to find out the secret words.

Writing Prompt

Pick an object in the room. Write a paragraph describing it to someone who can't see it. What words can you use to describe what it looks like and what it does?

Discussion Question

Many people in our society live with disabilities. Have you noticed anything in public places that makes it easier for people with disabilities? Do you think more could be done to make things accessible for people with disabilities? If so, what?

Links

 Helen Keller: Courage in the Dark by Johanna Hurwitz (Random House, 1997)

 Helen Keller Worldwide **www.hkworld.org/about_hkw/ helenkeller.html**

Key Vocabulary

communicate: to share ideas, thoughts, and feelings with another person

gestures: hand movements that communicate feelings or ideas

Susan B. Anthony's Vote for the Future

by Tracey West

★ ★ ★ ★ ★ ★ ★ ★ Characters ★ ★ ★ ★ ★ ★ ★ ★

Narrator 1
Narrator 2
Susan B. Anthony
Mary (Anthony's sister)
Voting Inspector 1

Voting Inspector 2
Deputy Marshal
Henry Selden (Anthony's lawyer)
Judge Hunt

SCENE 1

Narrator 1: Less than a hundred years ago, women in the United States did not have the right to vote.

Narrator 2: Women had to pay taxes. They had to obey laws. But they had no say in how the government was run.

Narrator 1: In the late 1800s, women began to fight for their rights. Susan B. Anthony was one of those women.

Susan B. Anthony: The Constitution says that citizens of the United States may enjoy the privileges of the United States. Well, women are citizens. And voting is a privilege. So women should have the right to vote.

Narrator 2: Susan B. Anthony decided to vote in the next election. Almost fifty other women in her town of Rochester, New York, decided to do the same.

Narrator 1: They took the first step on November 1, 1872. Anthony and her three sisters went to register to vote. The voting inspectors were set up in a barber shop.

Susan: We demand that you allow us to register to vote.

Voting Inspector 1: We can't do that. It is against the law for women to vote.

Mary: But the constitution says that all citizens of the United States have the same privileges. We just want the same privileges that men have.

Voting Inspector 2: The law is the law.

Susan: If you refuse to grant us our rights as citizens, I will take you all to court. I will sue each one of you!

Voting Inspector 1: Maybe we should talk to our supervisor.

Narrator 2: The voting inspectors allowed Susan B. Anthony and fourteen other women to register to vote that day.

SCENE 2

Narrator 1: Four days later, Susan B. Anthony cast a vote in the election.

Narrator 2: The voting inspectors accepted her vote. But some people in Rochester were not happy to hear that a woman had voted.

Narrator 1: A warrant was issued for Susan B. Anthony's arrest.

Narrator 2: On November 18, a United States deputy marshal went to Anthony's home to arrest her.

Mary: Susan, there is someone here to see you.

Deputy Marshal: Hello, Miss Anthony.

Susan: I have been expecting you.

Deputy Marshal: Nice weather we're having, isn't it?

Susan: Get to the point. Is this how you would arrest a man?

Deputy Marshal: Well no, it isn't.

Susan: I want to be arrested in the proper way. Please take me to jail right now. I am not ashamed of casting a vote!

Narrator 1: Anthony was charged with voting without having a lawful right to vote, because she was female.

Narrator 2: She was set free on bail. Then she waited four months for her trial.

SCENE 3

Henry Selden: My client would like to speak for herself, your honor.

Judge Hunt: I will not allow it.

Narrator 1: The lawyers argued their cases. Judge Hunt would not allow Anthony to speak.

Narrator 2: Judge Hunt read a verdict that he had written before he heard both sides of the case.

Judge Hunt: The Constitution does not give women the right to vote. Miss Anthony broke the law. She must be found guilty.

Susan: Your honor, I have something to say.

Judge Hunt: No!

Susan: You have trampled on my rights today. You talk about the law. Well, the law gives me the right to a fair trial. But everyone in this court is a man. How is that fair?

Judge Hunt: Please sit down! I am ready to give you your sentence. You must pay a fine of one hundred dollars.

Susan: I will never pay it!

Narrator 1: Susan B. Anthony never paid the fine.

Narrator 2: She kept fighting for women's rights until her death in 1906.

Narrator 1: Women did not get the right to vote until 1920. Susan B. Anthony never saw her dream become real.

Narrator 2: But women everywhere are grateful to her for her vote in 1872. It was a vote to make a better future for all women.

The End

Susan B. Anthony's Vote for the Future

Background

Susan B. Anthony was born in 1820 in Adams, Massachusetts. Born to a Quaker family, she grew up in an environment of activism and social change.

After teaching for 15 years, Anthony joined the temperance movement. When she wasn't allowed to speak at temperance rallies, she began to crusade for women's rights, befriending Elizabeth Cady Stanton, another important figure in the women's rights movement.

Anthony spent the rest of her life traveling around the country and speaking about causes she believed in: women's suffrage, the abolition of slavery, the right of women to own property and control their earnings. She campaigned for these and other causes until the end of her life in 1906.

Activity: A Vote for All?

Consider trying this activity *before* reading the play. Announce that you are going to allow the class to vote on something that will affect the entire class, such as what you will do for recess or what kind of song you will sing in music class. Then announce that only boys have the right to vote. Take the vote, excluding the girls.

After the vote, ask the girls: *How did you feel about not being able to vote? Was it fair? Why or why not?* Ask the boys how they felt about the situation. Explain that until 1920, women in this country did not have the right to vote. Use this as a springboard to reading the play.

You could also try variations on this activity. After the boys vote, announce that only certain boys can vote on the next question, such as those with brown eyes or boys wearing blue shirts. Continue until no one in your class has the right to vote.

Writing Prompt

Imagine that you can send a letter back in time to Susan B. Anthony. Write a letter telling her how the world has changed since she fought for women's rights.

Discussion Question

Susan B. Anthony did not live to see women get the right to vote. If she were alive today, how do you think she would feel about how women are treated? Do all people in today's society have equal rights?

Links

 Susan B. Anthony by Lucia Raatma (Compass Point Books, 2001)

 PBS: Not for Ourselves Alone: The Story of Elizabeth Cady Stanton and Susan B. Anthony
www.pbs.org/stantonanthony/

Key Vocabulary

privilege: a special right given to a person or group of people

verdict: the decision of a judge or jury about whether an accused person is guilty or innocent

Rosa Parks Leads the Way

by Tracey West

Characters

Narrator 1
Narrator 2
Young Rosa
Mother
Raymond Parks

Rosa Parks
Bus Driver
Police Officer
E. D. Nixon

SCENE 1

Narrator 1: On February 4, 1913, a little girl named Rosa was born on a farm in Alabama.

Narrator 2: Rosa's family was African American. Growing up, Rosa learned that some people in the South hated all people with dark skin.

Young Rosa:	Mama, what is that noise outside?
Mother:	That's the Ku Klux Klan, Rosa. They are riding tonight. It's not safe for black people when the Klan is out.
Young Rosa:	Why do they hate us?
Mother:	I don't know, Rosa. I don't know.
Narrator 1:	As Rosa grew up, it made her sad and angry that black people weren't treated fairly in the South.
Narrator 2:	Rosa married Raymond Parks in 1932. Raymond was an activist who fought for the rights of African Americans.
Raymond Parks:	We can make a difference, Rosa. I know things will change one day.
Narrator 1:	Rosa found work as a seamstress. She and Raymond also worked for the National Association for the Advancement of Colored People (NAACP) in Montgomery, Alabama.
Rosa Parks:	The NAACP does good work. But sometimes it seems like things will never change.

SCENE 2

Narrator 2:	Rosa didn't know it, but soon she would do something that would change history.
Narrator 1:	On December 1, 1955, Rosa got on the bus after working at a Montgomery department store. It had been a long day, and she was tired.
Bus Driver:	Get to the back of the bus!
Rosa:	*(to herself)* The law says that black people must sit in the back of the bus. It's so unfair. I am just lucky there is an empty seat.

Narrator 2: The bus made more stops, and more people got on. The bus driver saw that some white people could not find a seat.

Bus Driver: You, in the back! Stand up.

Narrator 1: Three other African Americans sitting in the back stood up. But Rosa was tired from working all day—more importantly, she was tired of following rules that were unfair.

Rosa: I will not.

Bus Driver: Get out of your seat, or I'll have you arrested!

Rosa: Then do that. I will not move.

Narrator 2: The bus driver stopped the bus. Two police officers got on.

Police Officer: Ma'am, why won't you just stand up? You know that colored people have to give up their seats to white people.

Rosa: I don't think I should have to stand up. The law is unfair. Why do you push us around?

Officer: The law is the law. You are under arrest.

Narrator 1: That is when Rosa finally stood up. The police officers took her off the bus and brought her to jail.

SCENE 3

Narrator 2: Mr. E. D. Nixon, a leader in the NAACP, came to see Rosa in jail.

E. D. Nixon: I can help get you out of jail, Rosa. But you have really started something here.

Rosa: What do you mean?

E.D.: I will be meeting with some of the leaders of the black community later. I think we can organize a boycott against the bus company. If we refuse to ride the buses, the law will have to change.

Rosa: Do you think that could really work?

Narrator 1: It took a year, but the boycott did its job. The bus company lost thousands of riders.

Narrator 2: The boycott got the attention of people all over the country. On December 20, 1956, the Supreme Court ruled that Montgomery's bus laws were unfair.

Narrator 1: From then on, black people could sit wherever they wanted on the bus. And that was just the beginning. Rosa's decision to stand up for herself marked the start of the Civil Rights Movement.

The End

Rosa Parks Leads the Way

Background

The Montgomery bus laws were not the only laws in the twentieth century that were unfair to blacks. In many places, African Americans could not find equal housing, drink from the same water fountain, eat in the same restaurants, or go to the same school as whites.

Rosa Parks's decision to remain seated on December 1, 1955, was the spark that led to the dissolution of these laws. After the Supreme Court victory in 1956, Parks remained active in the Civil Rights Movement. She gave speeches, attended marches, and with her husband founded the Rosa and Raymond Parks Institute for Self-Development to provide career training for young people. In 1999 she was awarded the Congressional Medal of Honor, the highest award a civilian can receive from the government.

Activity: Medal of Honor

Tell students that in 1999, Rosa Parks was awarded the Congressional Medal of Honor for helping to make the United States a better place to live for all people. Have students think about a person they think deserves a Medal of Honor for their service to the United States. (You may wish to allow children time to research this, or assign it as a take-home project.)

Have students write a paragraph explaining why the person they chose deserves a medal. Affix the paragraphs to construction paper and allow students to draw a picture of the person they chose on the top half of the page. Finally, have students cut out yellow construction paper circles for medals and affix them to the corner of the page. Consider displaying the medal winners on a wall or bulletin board.

Writing Prompt

Do you have a question you'd like to ask Rosa Parks, or would you like to tell her how you feel about what she did? Write your questions or feelings in a letter. (Check the Girl Power! Web site to find an address to send your letter to Rosa Parks.)

Discussion Question

How would it make you feel if you were not allowed to sit on a bus, or eat in a restaurant, just because of the color of your skin? How do you think African-American people felt before these laws were changed?

Links

 If a Bus Could Talk: The Story of Rosa Parks by Faith Ringgold (Simon & Schuster, 1999)

 Girl Power! Guests: Spotlight on Mrs. Rosa Parks
www.girlpower.gov/girlarea/gpguests/RosaParks.htm

Key Vocabulary

boycott: to refuse to buy or pay to use something as an act of protest

civil rights: the rights that all people have to be treated equally under law

NAACP: National Association for the Advancement of Colored People

Remembering Dr. King

by Tracey West

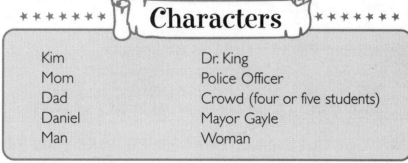

Characters

Kim	Dr. King
Mom	Police Officer
Dad	Crowd (four or five students)
Daniel	Mayor Gayle
Man	Woman

SCENE 1

Kim: I can't believe that today everyone in America will celebrate the birthday of Dr. Martin Luther King, Jr.

Mom: It took almost twenty years for this day to come.

Dad: Dr. King was born on January 15, 1928, but our country will celebrate the holiday every year on the third Monday in January.

Daniel: I can't wait for the parade!

Kim: I hope we get to learn about Dr. King. Did you and Daddy ever see him?

Mom: I saw him on television when I was a little girl. But I bet some of the people here at this parade have met Dr. King.

Man: I don't mean to interrupt you. But I can tell you about Dr. King. I was there in 1956, the day his house got bombed.

Daniel: Somebody bombed his house? Why would they do that?

Dad: Dr. King was leading a movement to change laws in Montgomery, Alabama, that were unfair to blacks. And some people hated him for it.

Man: That's right. I'll never forget that day. We were so angry. But Dr. King kept the peace.

SCENE 2

Dr. King: What's happened here? My wife, my baby girl—are they all right?

Police Officer: They're fine. The bomb didn't hurt them.

Crowd: Do something! This isn't fair! This isn't right!

Mayor Gayle: Calm down, everyone. Go home. We will take care of this.

Crowd: We won't go! That bomb could have killed Dr. King and his family.

Dr. King: Please calm down. My wife and baby are all right. I am all right. We can't respond to violence with violence. We must act peacefully.

SCENE 3

Man: I'll never forget that day. Dr. King taught me that evil could be fought with peace, not violence.

Dad: Dr. King led many peaceful demonstrations to protest the unfair treatment of blacks.

Mom: He and others were often attacked. But they never gave up.

Dad: In 1964, Dr. King won the Nobel Peace Prize for his work.

Woman: Excuse me, but I heard you talking. I have a story about Dr. King too. I was there for the March on Washington.

Daniel: I know about that! Thousands of people marched to the Lincoln Memorial in Washington, D.C.

Kim: Did you really hear Dr. King's famous speech?

Woman: There were more than 200,000 of us in that crowd, and his words moved all of us.

SCENE 4

Dr. King: I have a dream that my four little children will one day live in a nation where they will not be judged by the color of their skin but by the content of their character.

I have a dream today.

I have a dream that one day the state of Alabama . . . will be transformed into a situation where little black boys and black girls will be able to join hands with little white boys and white girls and walk together as sisters and brothers.

SCENE 5

Woman: People all over the world believed in Dr. King's dream.

Mom: He worked every day of his life to make the world a better place for all of us.

Kim: Dr. King's dream was a good one. Why was he killed because of it?

Dad: Not everyone believed in that dream. That's why it's important for us to keep his dream alive.

Daniel: I'll never forget this parade today.

Kim: I'm glad his birthday is a national holiday. Now we can always remember Dr. King.

The End

Remembering Dr. King

Background

After his tragic death in 1968, bills to make Dr. King's birthday a national holiday were introduced in Congress, but none passed. The lobbying effort continued until 1983, when the House approved the measure, and the Senate followed suit after President Ronald Reagan promised to sign the bill. The first official year of the holiday was 1986.

The creation of the holiday is a powerful testament to Dr. King's legacy. He is the only American besides George Washington and Abraham Lincoln whose birthday is celebrated as a national holiday. When the holiday was announced, Civil Rights leaders expressed the hope that the day would be one in which Dr. King's beliefs and principles would always be remembered.

Activity: Mural of Dreams

To make this mural, you'll need a roll of white paper (found in art supply or teacher supply stores). Unroll the paper to the desired length—from three to six feet should work well. In the center of the paper, write the words *I Have a Dream*. Discuss with the class the dream of Dr. Martin Luther King, Jr. What was his vision for a better world? What are some other ways we could make the world a better place? Provide children with paints, markers, or crayons and ask them to draw their dream for a better world. Hang the finished mural on the wall or in a hallway.

Writing Prompt

What is your dream for the world? In what ways would it help people? Describe your dream and what steps you could take to make it a reality.

Discussion Question

What do you think Dr. King meant when he said he wanted people to be judged not "by the color of their skin but by the content of their character"?

Links

 Happy Birthday, Martin Luther King by Jean Marzollo (Scholastic, 1993)

 Seattle Times: Martin Luther King, Jr. http://seattletimes.nwsource.com/mlk/index.html

Key Vocabulary

demonstration: a gathering of people who are protesting something

transformed: changed

Neil Armstrong
Man on the Moon

by Tracey West

***** Characters *****

Narrator 1	Edwin E. "Buzz" Aldrin Jr.
Narrator 2	Michael Collins
Flight Instructor	Charles Duke
Neil Armstrong	

SCENE 1

Narrator 1: Let's go back in time to 1946. We're in a small town in Ohio.

Flight Instructor: Congratulations, Neil! You've earned your pilot's license.

Neil Armstrong: I said I would get my pilot's license on my sixteenth birthday, and I meant it.

**Flight
Instructor:** So what's next for Neil Armstrong?

Neil: I am going to join the military as soon as I'm old enough. I want to study flight, and fly planes for a living.

**Flight
Instructor:** I'm sure you'll go far, Neil.

SCENE 2

Narrator 2: Now let's take a giant leap to the year 1969. Neil Armstrong achieved his goals.

Narrator 1: Neil flew a fighter plane in the Korean War. He tested planes for the National Aeronautics and Space Administration (NASA). But now he was about to take his most important flight ever.

**Buzz:
Aldrin:** Mmm, steak and eggs. A breakfast fit for an astronaut.

**Michael
Collins:** It's the last good meal we're going to get for a long time.

Neil: That's right. So as your commander, I order you to clean your plate.

Michael: I can't believe that in three days we'll be orbiting the moon.

Buzz: And walking on its surface.

Michael: You and Neil get to take the first moon walk. I'll be waiting for you in the command module.

Neil: We're not even sure if we'll be able to walk on the moon when we get there. Nobody knows exactly what to expect.

Buzz: We'll know soon enough. It's almost time to launch!

SCENE 3

Narrator 2: On July 16, 1969, Neil Armstrong, Buzz Aldrin, and Michael Collins blasted off toward the moon.

Narrator 1: Four days later, the command module, Columbia, was orbiting the moon. Neil Armstrong and Buzz Aldrin climbed into the Eagle, which was attached to Columbia.

Michael: You cats take it easy on the lunar surface.

Buzz: Okay, Mike.

Narrator 2: The Eagle broke away from Columbia.

Neil: The Eagle has wings!

Narrator 1: Neil piloted the Eagle to a safe landing on the moon's surface.

Narrator 2: Neil told the good news to Charles Duke, the communicator at the space center in Houston, Texas.

Neil: Houston, the Eagle has landed!

Charles Duke: Roger, we copy. It was beautiful from here. There are a lot of smiling faces in this room, and all over the world.

Neil: There are two of them up here.

Michael: And don't forget one in the command module!

SCENE 4

Narrator 1: Back on Earth, millions of people watched the moon landing on live television.

Narrator 2: But the most exciting part of the journey was about to happen.

Neil: The dust is settling out there. There sure are a lot of rocks and craters.

Buzz: Let's get on our outdoor suits. We won't have much time out there.

Narrator 1: Neil and Buzz opened the hatch. Neil climbed down a ladder leading to the moon's surface.

Narrator 2: Neil placed his left foot, then his right, on the moon. Then he let go of the ladder.

Neil: That's one small step for a man, one giant leap for mankind!

Narrator 1: Buzz Aldrin stepped on the moon a few minutes later. Others have followed in the footsteps of these astronauts.

Narrator 2: But the world will never forget Neil Armstrong, the first man to walk on the moon.

The End

Neil Armstrong
Man on the Moon

Background

Neil Armstrong was not the first man to travel to space—that honor belongs to Russian cosmonaut Yury Gagarin—but he does hold the distinction of being the first human being to set foot on the moon. Armstrong traveled to the moon on the Apollo 11 mission in 1969, with astronauts Michael Collins and Buzz Aldrin. Armstrong joined the space program in 1962, after studying aeronautical engineering at Purdue University, flying fighter planes in the Korean War, and flight testing supersonic aircraft for NASA.

Neil Armstrong's famous words, "That's one small step for a man, one giant leap for mankind," will go down in history. However, we should note that the quote came through the transmission as "That's one small step for man," which changes the meaning of the quote. Armstrong contends that the word "a" was lost in a transmission glitch.

Activity: Moonwalk Matching Game

Create a variation on a traditional matching game using words and definitions about the moonwalk. First write the names of five to ten space or moon related words on plain 3" x 5" index cards. Then write a definition for each word on a separate card. Use words from the Key Vocabulary list, plus any you'd like to add (such as *planet, moon, rocket,* and *Neil Armstrong*).

Use the cards to play a matching game. Put the word cards face down on a table in the shape of a square or rectangle. Then place the definition cards face down to form another square. To play the game, have players take turns picking one card from each pile. If the word and definition match, they get to keep the cards. If the cards do not match, they must put the cards back down on the table and the next player gets a turn. The player who holds the most cards at the end of the game is the winner.

Writing Prompt

Think about a time when you saw the moon in the night sky. Write a paragraph describing what the moon looks like from Earth.

Discussion Question

What do you think Neil Armstrong meant when he said, "That's one small step for a man, one giant leap for mankind"?

Links

 One Giant Leap: The Story of Neil Armstrong by Don Brown (Houghton Mifflin, 2001)

 NASA Kids
http://kids.msfc.nasa.gov/news/1999/news-apollo11.asp

Key Vocabulary

astronaut: someone who travels in space

orbit: to travel around a planet, the moon, the sun, etc.

module: a separate section that can be linked to other parts

lunar: having to do with the moon

NASA: National Aeronautics and Space Administration

Notes

Notes